UNDERSTANDING CREDIT
Made Simple

Say Goodbye To Debt Forever

Dr. Rosie Milligan
Credit Consultant, Senior Estate Planner

Professional Publishing House
1425 W. Manchester Ave., Ste. B
Los Angeles, California 90047
323-750-3592
Email: professionalpublishinghouse@yahoo.com
www.Professionalpublishinghouse.com

Cover design: TWA Solutions.com
First printing December 2016
978-0-9983089-0-6
10987654321

For inquiries contact: Drrosie@aol.com

FOOD FOR THOUGHT

As a credit consultant, I provide credit consultation to clients nationwide. There are many who can help you write letters to the credit bureaus, disputing the inaccurate and erroneous information on your credit profile. I take you beyond dispute letters; I educate you on how to rebuild good credit and maintain it forever.

If you are struggling to pay off your debts, in the appendix, I have provided you with *21 Ways To Save Money To Pay Down Your Debts Without Increasing Your Income.*

Dr. Rosie Milligan, Senior Estate Planner and Credit Consultant
1425 W. Manchester Ave. Ste. B, Los Angeles, California 90047
Phone: 323-750-3592
Email: drrosie@aol.com
website: Drrosie.com

Books On Business & Finance
by Dr. Rosie Milligan

1. Getting Out Of Debt Made Simple

2. Understanding Credit Made Simple

3. Creating A Budget Made Simple

4. What You Need To Know Before You
   Start A Business

5. Departing This Life Preparations:
   Everything You Need To Know To
   Get Your Personal And   Business
   Affairs In Order

*For other books by Dr. Rosie
Milligan, visit Drrosie.com.*

Good credit is like insurance, you don't wait until you need it to try and get it.

***

Credit is better than cash these days.

***

Your credit is liken to your vital signs, you should monitor it often.

Table of Contents

Chapter 1

CREDIT IS BETTER THAN HAVING CASH THESE DAYS

When it comes to getting a job, leasing/buying/renting a car, buying a house, or renting an apartment, credit is more important than having cash. We are living in a FICO system society and credit really matters. You can have money in the bank, credit cards in your wallet, and still get rejected when trying to rent a house, apartment, or car when your credit report is pulled.

It's time to be proactive. Get your credit score in order *now*. Don't wait for multiple rejections before you act. Stop paying too much for everything you buy. You do not have to live that way—become a "GAME" changer and live life on your terms. Others have done so, and you can also with having the right information. Every financial decision made today is based on your FICO score. It is unfortunate that most people have no clue what their FICO is nor what it means.

You will need to improve your credit score immediately, if:

1. You are job seeking.

2. You plan to purchase a car or home and want a decent interest rate and a lower monthly payment.

3. Your auto lease is expiring soon.

4. You are looking to rent a house, apartment, or car.

5. You want to lower your car insurance.

6. You are due for an employee review on certain government jobs.

Chapter 2

UNDERSTANDING THE NEW FICO CREDIT SCORING SYSTEM

What is a FICO Score and What Does it Stand For?

A FICO score is a credit score developed by Fair Issac Corporation, a company specializing in what's known as "predictive analytics," which means they take information and analyze it to predict what's likely to happen.

In the case of credit scores, FICO looks at a range of credit information and uses that to create scores that help lenders predict consumer behavior, such as how likely someone is to pay their bills on time (or not), or whether they are able to handle a larger credit line.

Prior to 2000, having good credit was much simpler. If you had established credit accounts and paid your creditors on time, you would have a good credit rating. Furthermore, it was fashionable to open your wallet and roll out ten or more credit cards you were using monthly, and as long as you paid them on time, the limit/balance on your card did not impact your credit score.

The FICO credit scoring model was thrust upon the world in 2000. Most people are not aware that we have a completely different credit system now than we had prior to the ushering in of the FICO system. The single biggest problem today with credit restoration is that people are still using old-system techniques to correct new-system problems.

The credit breakdown under the new credit scoring FICO system is as follows:

- Types of credit used = 10%,

- Length of credit history = 15%,
- Amount owed = 30%,
- Inquiries about new credit = 10%,
- Payment history = 35%.

You can have six major credit cards and pay them all on time. However, charging more than 35% of your available balance on those cards can reduce your FICO score. Remember, under the old credit system, this would not have hurt your credit points. Maxing your credit cards to the limit could appear as if all your credit cards are tapped out, you are not financially stable and you are surviving off your credit cards. Also, should you become unable to work/operate your business, your financial status will collapse.

Chapter 3

WHEN IT COMES TO CREDIT, FINANCIAL LITERACY IS KEY

Financial literacy, which includes a basic understanding of how credit works, is key to financial stability and economic empowerment throughout the world. Unfortunately, a person can complete a four-year college degree and have no knowledge of how credit works, and have no clue about the word FICO. Usually, their first encounter with the words FICO and credit score are introduced to them when they are approved or denied for credit.

Today, your credit score is likened to your vital signs. It's being monitored at all times, and yet, most people don't know their credit score. About 43 million Americans have a credit score of 599 or less. Many, who discover their credit score, do not have knowledge of what can be done regarding their credit report if there are errors on their report. The Credit Reporting Act gives Americans the right to dispute and investigate any item on their credit report. There are inaccurate, erroneous, and obsolete items on people's credit report that can be removed via the proper channel. Unfortunately, some people have been rejected for credit due to inaccurate or erroneous items on their credit report, which is the reason for routinely checking your credit report prior to attempting to secure a loan or making a purchase on credit.

Credit Bureaus

There are three credit bureaus: Equifax, Experian, and TransUnion. These bureaus are privately held, billion-dollar companies. They do not verify items placed on your credit reports. They pay fines each year for failing to update credit files correctly. They don't make money correcting credit, they make it selling credit files to big industries and companies.

Let's take a look at the Credit Score Grades:

720 and above = very good

675–719 = good

621–674 = fair

620–below = poor

You may find that each credit bureau may have a different score for your credit. When you take a look at your credit report from the different credit bureaus, you will note that some of your credit accounts are not listed with each credit bureau. If companies/businesses subscribe/report to different credit bureaus, an account may be on one bureau and not on the other two. When pulling your credit report, be sure to pull from all three credit bureaus. You may pull your credit once a year at no charge, from all bureaus.

Chapter 4

THE IMPACT OF NEGATIVE ITEMS ON YOUR CREDIT REPORT

Negative items on your credit report can impact your ability to obtain credit and can cause you to have to pay a higher interest rate if approved for credit. There are state and federal laws that govern the length of time negative items can remain on your credit report. This is vital information, particularly when you are trying to restore your credit.

The following negative items generally can remain on your credit report:

- Delinquencies: May remain up to seven years from the date of the initial missed payment.

- Collection Accounts: May remain up to seven years from the date of the initial missed payment that led to the collection. When a collection account is paid in full, its status on your credit report will be updated to Paid Collection.

- Charged-Off Accounts: May remain up to seven years from the date of the initial missed payment that led to the charge-off, even if the payments are later made on the account.

- Closed Accounts: May remain up to seven years from the date they are reported closed. A positive closed account may remain up to ten years.

- Bankruptcies: Chapters 7, 11, and 12 may remain up to ten years from the filing date. Chapter 13 may remain up to seven years from the filing date. **Accounts included in bankruptcy may remain up to seven years from the date they were reported as included in the bankruptcy.**

- Child Support Judgments: May remain up to seven years from the filing date.

- Tax Liens: If unpaid, may remain up to fifteen years from the filing date. Paid tax liens may remain up to seven years from the date paid.

- Civil and Small Claims Judgments: May remain up to seven years from the filing date.

- Inquiries: May remain up to two years.

Points to remember that will help you when attempting to stabilize your credit.

1. Every state has Statute of Limitation laws. The time limit for each state may differ, therefore, you want to check it for the state that

you live in. Statute of Limitation laws limit the time that a debt can be pursued for collection in a court of law. This does not mean that the creditor debt is discharged and they cannot continue to pursue attempting to collect on what's owed to them. It only means they cannot bring it into the court of law for collection.

2. Every major creditor in this country has a Hardship Program. Do not allow them to get away with telling you that they do not have this program. There are

several things a creditor can do to help you, such as: reduce the principle amount, reduce interest, and reduce the monthly payment amount. The government has given incentives to creditors for helping to eliminate consumers' debts.

Elimination of debt is important to our government. When consumers cannot purchase automobiles and houses, our economy suffers badly and will be in danger of collapsing.

Chapter 5

A REFLECTION OF CREDIT, PAST AND PRESENT

Banking and Credit

You have always needed good credit to borrow money from a bank, but now, you actually need good credit to *give* banks money. Almost every bank or lending institution will do a credit check prior to opening a savings or checking account for you.

Housing and Credit

You have always needed good credit to buy a house, but now you need good credit in order to *rent* a house "almost any place.." There are very few places left in this country where you can live without passing a credit check. Today, there are people with good jobs and money in the bank who cannot rent a house or apartment due to poor credit, causing many of them to rent neighborhood motels for their family housing.

Employment and Credit

Nearly every job, even those that pay minimum wage, requires a credit check of some type. This is new under the FICO system. Some employers do a random credit check for employees, and employees are subject to lose their jobs based on their credit report.

Insurance and Credit

If you were to ask, "What is the single greatest factor that determines your car insurance rates?" most people would say zip code or your driving record. Both answers would be incorrect. The single greatest factor that determines your auto insurance rate is *your credit score.*

A Note Regarding Student Loans

I would be remiss if I did not mention student loans. Student loans are a major problem for many, young and old. There are many parents who are paying for student loans, which they cosigned for. If you are responsible for a student loan debt that is in default, your Social Security check can be garnished in the amount of 15% of your monthly check. Student loan liability can cause one's credit score to be lowered. There are many good reasons for a student to not be able to repay a student loan. However, it is important to be in contact with your creditor regarding your student loan. Ignoring your student loan is not a good idea, even if you are disabled at the time and are unable to pay. There are provisions for the disabled and for those who just cannot make payments due to hardships, etc.

The headlines of a Special ABC News report, on April 4, 2015, read:

22 States Where You Could Lose Your License for Not Paying Your Student Loans.

Failing to repay student loans has all sorts of terrible consequences, but in some states, more than just your financial well-being is at risk—student loan default could cost you your professional certification or even your driver's license.

Chapter 6

WHY CREDIT RESTORATION IS IMPORTANT TODAY

Nearly every financial decision is based on your credit score. Therefore, it is important to restore your credit based on the new credit system. We all know the cost of poor credit is too high. We hear more about the FICO score than we have ever heard before and everything is FICO driven.

In an era where there is a job shortage and employees are being denied jobs as well as being terminated from jobs due to poor credit, it has become an urgent need to have credit restored. There are many companies springing up, as well as individuals who profess to have the ability to, as they call it, "Fix Credit." However, many of those who advertise they can fix your credit are doing so using the old credit system while trying to fix a new credit problem. You want to work with a company that specializes in Credit Restoration, utilizing strategies applicable to the new FICO score system. And you want to seek assistance from a company with at least five years or more of credit restoration experience.

Increasing your credit score will give you access to capital, and you will pay less interest on your purchases, including your car insurance. A low credit score can cause one to pay more interest on all purchases, and paying higher interest for everything is like riding down the freeway and throwing $400 per month out of your car window.

Credit will impact four areas in your life: housing, banking, employment, and insurance. Having bad credit can cost you over $200,000 during a lifetime. Below is an example of two students paying a student loan of $8,000 with different interest rates.

- Karen's interest rate is 7.25%, her monthly payment is $234, and her total interest paid in ten years is $8,175.

- Joyce has bad credit; her interest rate is 13.25% on an $8,000 loan. Her monthly payment is $302 per month, and her total interest paid in ten years is $16,189. Joyce's penalty for having bad credit is $8,013.

Become proactive and prepare now. Don't wait until you need credit to check to see what your credit status is—check now. We are living in a time when it's better to have credit than cash. You can have $30,000 in the bank and you can be denied the rental of an apartment, house, or car. Remember, what you have in your bank account says nothing about how well you pay your bills. We have moved to a "plastic" society with most transactions done via credit cards. People are even paying rent online via credit cards. **GONE ARE THE DAYS WHEN PEOPLE WHO HAD CASH COULD SAY, "I DON'T NEED CREDIT, I HAVE CASH!"**

Bad Credit Can Cost You:

1. The job you always want.

2. The apartment or home you want to rent.

3. High interest rates when purchasing a car.

4. Higher insurance rates.

A Word of Caution

Many car rental businesses are doing a credit check when you use a debit card versus a credit card for means of payment.

DO NOT BE SCAMMED BY INEXPERIENCED CREDIT REPAIR COMPANIES!

Do your homework before signing the contract to have your credit restored.

I strongly recommend you read my book, *Getting Out Of Debt Made Simple*. It will teach you how to save money without increasing your income. You will learn 75 ways to save money, and the money you save can be used to pay off your debts. The book also includes a detailed budget plan.

STOP BEING A "SLAVE" TO DEBT AND GET OUT OF DEBTOR'S PRISON, NOW!

Chapter 7

SOME MYTHS ABOUT CREDIT REPORTS

You are not alone if you think the credit reporting process is complicated—millions of Americans share that same feeling.

With the various credit bureaus, endless credit reporting rules and laws, and more than enough websites advertising "free" credit scores and reports, it can be difficult for the average consumer to completely understand what is included in a credit report, how the information is reported and what effect it has on the credit score. Because of these and many other factors, individuals often turn to the Internet and people they know to get answers to their questions regarding their credit report.

It's okay to do your research, but take caution and consider your sources. There is a lot of misinformation on the web regarding what your credit reports actually mean. Here are some of the most common myths to look out for.

No Need to Check Your Report If You Pay Your Bills On Time

Many people assume that if they're paying their bills on time, there is no need to check their credit reports. However, fraudulent activity or computer error can cause a negative mark on your report and checking the report is the only way to find out.

Checking Your Own Report Hurts Your Score

It helps to understand the difference between a hard credit check (hard inquiry) and a soft one. A hard inquiry is when **lenders** review your credit information. Doing so multiple times can have a negative impact on your score.

A soft check of your credit (soft inquiry) does not have any impact on your credit. Soft checks allow individuals to review or monitor their own credit and it also allows employers, lenders, landlords, and others to access limited data from the report.

Paying Off A Debt Removes It From The Credit Report

Many borrowers become disappointed when they pay off a debt, only to learn that it doesn't automatically come off of their credit report. Negative entries are usually taken off every seven years and as many as ten years for foreclosures, serious delinquencies, or bankruptcies. However, inaccurate negative items should be discussed with the credit reporting agency immediately.

Debt Only Occurs On The Report In One Entry

If you have a delinquent debt that has been sold to a collection agency, both can place the debt on your credit report, resulting in two negative items on the report.

Cancelling An Old Credit Card May Hurt Your Credit History

This is one of the largest myths out there. Canceling the oldest credit card you have won't have a negative impact on your credit. Closed accounts stay on your reports longer than negative entries.

However, choosing to close a credit card that carries a large credit limit when you have outstanding debt could affect the utilization ratio of your credit.

APPENDIX

21 Ways To Save Money Without Increasing Your Income

1. Purchase a cell phone where there is no charge to you for incoming calls.

2. Do not allow your gasoline tank drop below a quarter of a tank; your car uses more gas when this occurs, and this can also lead to a burned-out fuel pump.

3. Use Google search for telephone numbers versus dialing 411, which costs.

4. Plan a weekly menu. Make a grocery

list before grocery shopping. When shopping, stick to your list.

5. Learn ways to create a new dish from leftovers and make it taste fresh & new.

6. Use shopping coupons when grocery shopping.

7. Do bulk shopping with a family member/friend when purchasing items such as toilet tissue, paper towels, Kleenex, etc.

8. Wash a full load of clothes when washing versus everybody in the house washing a few pieces at a time.

9. Save on gasoline by mapping out your travel route before you get started each day with errands/chores.

10. Purchase automobile insurance with a $500–$1,000 deductible. As you know, in most cases, people do not report damage under $500 for fear of an insurance rate increase— so why pay extra?

11. Pay off credit cards with the highest interest rates first or switch outstanding credit cards with a high interest rate to a card with a low interest rate. Place the interest saved in a savings account.

12. Purchase items like an electric heater or fan during off-season when they are less expensive.

13. Recycle bottles, cans, etc. A little can add up to a lot, and you will be quite surprised about how much money your recycling can turn into.

14. Invest in a water system rather than buying single bottles of water. It will pay off in the long run.

15. Do not discard purses and shoes that can be repaired. Take them to a shoe repair shop.

16. Eat leftovers for lunch.

17. Repair leaky faucets and any other water drippings.

18. Purchase an outside sensor light instead of leaving the porch light burning all night.

19. Weather-strip your windows and doors.

20. Find an honest mechanic and have your car serviced. The minute you hear unusual noises or sounds, have your car checked out. Learn how to check your engine oil and change it periodically. *It's cheaper to fix a little problem before it turns into*

a big problem. Your car is the next largest investment after your home, and you will need a car most of your life, so treat it like an investment—watch over it and manage it well.

21.   **Tips for saving at the gas pump**. (1) Slow your roll, speed eats up your fuel. Driving 5 miles over 60 mph, is like paying .30 extra for every gallon of gas you burn. (2)Do not load you car down with items such as: flags, bikes, carriers, luggage, racks, etc. Excess weight makes the engine work harder, increases drag which causes wasting of fuel.   Close your

car window when driving at high speed, this causes drag and wasting of fuel too. (3)Be a smooth operator. Avoid jerking, frequent accelerating when trying to go around and pass other vehicles and frequent jamming on your brakes. This alone can save you $1.00 or more per gallon of gasoline---this can make a financial difference. (4)Avoid idling of your car; 15 minutes of idling can burn a quarter of a gallon of gasoline.

Don't be afraid to get your hands a little dirty. Learn to check and to change your wiper blades, check belts and hoses for wear, clean the dirt and dust from the engine's air-filter, the dirt and dust clogs up the filter and causes the car to use more gasoline.

EACH ONE MUST TEACH ONE.

— Dr. Rosie Milligan

Order Form

BOOKS ON FINANCE BY DR. ROSIE MILLIGAN

TITLE	PRICE		QTY		TOTAL
Getting Out of Debt Made Simple	$10.00	x	___	=	_____
Understanding Credit Made Simple	$10.00	x	___	=	_____
Creating A Budget Made Simple	$5.00	x	___	=	_____
What You Need To Know Before You Start A Business	$15.00	x	___	=	_____
Departing This Life Preparations: Everything	$12.00	x	___	=	_____

You Need To Know To Get Your Personal & Business Affairs In Order

Shipping: **$6.45**
(add $1.00 each add'l book)

TOTAL DUE   _____

Payment/Customer Information

$_____ Due in check or money order

Name: _____
Address: _____
City: _____ State: _____ ZIP: _____
Phone: _____
E-mail: _____

Send Order Form and Payment to:

Professional Publishing House
1425 W. Manchester Ave., Ste. B
Los Angeles, California 90047